PRODUCTIVITY GENIUS

SUPER Productivity Techniques
That Built My Business to 6 Figures

Bonus! - As a way of saying thanks, here's a short book that is guaranteed to excel your business career. It helped me greatly and will do the same for you if you can internalise the concepts.

Download Here → *http://goo.gl/iYx5aC*

Join Our Insider List

Get Our Premium Books Below for Only 99 Cents!

Join Here ^   http://goo.gl/wcNCvW

Insiders get Discounts to our Upcoming Book Titles upon Book Launch.

<u>COMING SOON</u>

QUTTING WORK TO START A BUSINESS IN 2016

From a SIX Figure Entrepreneur who did Exactly That

Written By:

Mateen Soudagar

Brought to you by AffEngineer.com

www.AffEngineer.com Copyright © 2015 by AffEngineer Publishing

Disclaimer

No part of this publication may be reproduced or transmitted in any form or by any means, mechanical or electronic, including photocopying or recording, or by any information storage and retrieval system, or transmitted by email without permission in writing from the publisher.

While all attempts have been made to verify the information provided in this publication, neither the author nor the publisher assumes any responsibility for errors, omissions or contrary interpretations of the subject matter herein.

This book is for entertainment purposes only. The views expressed are those of the author alone, and should not be taken as expert instruction or commands. The reader is responsible for his or her own actions.

Adherence to all applicable laws and regulations, including international, federal,

Introduction

Productivity is a lot more complex then people think. It's only when you start giving it the respect and time it needs to develop that you start to see improvements in your business ventures.

Being productive at work is one thing when the boss is down your throat but when you work for yourself and you have the choice to be productive or not, it's a whole different ball game.

I never had issues with productivity at the start of business journey. Now, I'm 3 years in and am able to generate a nice stable income that's more than my engineering salary. I can maintain this easily by working less than 5 hours a week. At the start, I was desperate, had no income so it was easier to push myself to work more. As my income increased it became be hard to push myself on continuously expanding my income streams and business in general.

It was at this point I started looking for ways to improve my productivity. I experimented with everything under the sun and have realised you can definitely be more productive, it's all about implementing small but significant rules that keep you working.

Punishment for not working/doing a Certain Activity

When you have a job you may not realise it but the main reason you're able to get up and do things is because there's a consequence if you don't. If you get caught out lazing one too many times you'll get called into the office and if it continues, chances are, you'll lose your job.

When you work for yourself, you're your own boss. You can't really fire yourself so most people have a hard time keeping this pressure so they're able to work.

You have to treat yourself as both an employee and an employer because essentially that's what you are. You're a commander to yourself, a grinder, a leader, a labourer, all in one. You need to be able to switch between the two modes.

The best way to do this is to define roles for each. As an employer you give yourselves things to do and punish yourself for not following through. As an employee you will do the tasks given to you, (by yourself), or suffer the consequence of not doing them. I know it sounds weird and a little confusing but that's what we are. We're entrepreneurs and we do things differently. That's why we achieve things people only dream of achieving.

Give yourself some rules. If you break them punish yourself.

Punishments can come in many forms. It could be as simple as donating $50 to a charity you DON'T want to donate to. Yes, you read that correctly. Give that $50 to someone you trust and tell them to donate this to a charity you've specified if you tell them you didn't do the task(s) you needed to.

Whatever the punishment is, it should be something you REALLY don't want to do. Don't just pick something easy like put $2 in your piggy bank or give yourself a slap on the list. The punishment has to be so bad that thinking of it makes you cringe just like how you'd feel if you lost your job.

I've tried this multiple times in my life, each time it increased my productivity drastically. Once was when I vowed to not work on my business a whole day if I didn't do the tasks I had set myself to do. They only took 2-3 hours so it wasn't that I couldn't achieve them. Not being able to work on my business is a huge thing for me. At any given moment I'll be spending from $100 to $1000's a day on FaceBook advertising. You can imagine how many times I need to check my statistics to make sure everything is running smoothly. A small blunder can cost me a lot of money so I have to continuously monitor things.

To not be able to do this for a whole day is bad. It made me feel sick with paranoia and there was no way I could let myself do this. Guess what ended up happening? I skipped a day, just because I got a little lazy and thought I'd not follow through with the punishment. Employer me had other plans. He kept the punishment and for a whole day I wasn't able to do anything related to my business. Not even log in and monitor sales or answer crucial emails.

It was such a crappy helpless feeling that after that day I stuck to my tasks for the whole period till I changed my business model.

Like I said, you're an employer AND employee. It's a healthy balance of both. You can't just be an employer who writes a to do list and does no work and you can't just be an employee who grinds it out never really looking back to see if they're sticking to their over all plans and goals.

I have a friend who started a real estate business. At the start of it all it was pretty difficult. He was paid on commission and had to do a certain number of door knocks, cold calls, letter drops and a bunch of things no one really wants to do. He'd do it here and there and never get anywhere with the whole thing.

This is where I stepped in and told him about this technique. I told him I'd take his phone off him for a whole day if he fails to do 20 letter drops, 20 door knocks and 5 cold calls. At the start he was hesitant but later agreed. I never saw such a change in someone in a single day as I have with him. He was up and ready to go every day. He knew I'd follow through with my promise of taking the phone off him. He's a good friend and I go over often. He done it for months and made more sales then he ever did before.

I know it sounds scary punishing yourself like this but you need this type of pressure to get you to where you want to be. Sure, you may miss out on a $2,000 real estate deal by not having your phone for a day but you'll develop long term healthy habits that will get you plenty more deals in the future. Entrepreneurship is all about personal development and you have to go to the extreme to force yourself out of the comfort zone that keeps you from this development. Try this, it's a great technique for someone who can follow through with it.

Reward for Achieving a Goal

This time we're talking about the opposite.

It's easy to get carried away when you switch to working for yourself from working a full-tim job. You'll take holidays, say yes every time your friend calls you out and basically open all boundaries you had when you were working full-time.

Why wouldn't you? You've finally got the freedom to do what you want it's only natural to when to escape all the time. It takes some time to realise that this work won't get done by itself. Most business fail because people aren't able to spend the necessary time to build them at the start.

At the start, business is a grind. You nccd to bc able to work long hours till you get to where you want. Every outspoken entrepreneur that travels the world and always seems to have a lot of fun worked 12 hour days for days on end at some point. They slept in their cars, operated on little to no food, forgot to eat 3 meals in a row and basically worked like maniacs.

Even I turned into a half zombie during the early stages of my business. It's only later on when you get some income coming in that you should be rewarding yourself.

Don't let yourself buy all the new things you want or to go on holidays unless you're rewarding yourself. It's good to have fun and let loose sometimes but if you want to go on a holiday at the end of the year, tell yourself you're only allowed to go if you hit a certain target. The target could be financial or some other KPI. Whatever it is, make it measurable.

I set rewards like this all the time. They're kind of like bonuses. Remember, you're an employer as well as an employee!

I reward myself with clothe shopping sprees, car rims and aesthetic upgrades even holidays I go on, I only book if I achieve the goals I need to.

Some people work really well with this technique, some work really well with the punishment technique before this one. Whatever it is, you only realise through experimentation. Again, give it a go and see how your mind and body reacts.

No Social Media till you Finish Work

Emails and messages from people are really just HUH requests for your time.

Read that again till it settles in a bit.

People hardly contact you with something important, you don't NEED to respond straight away. I've learned to keep all my social media including FaceBook, Instagram, Snapchat, email, etc, all till after I finish work.

I'll see notifications pop up on my iPhone but I won't click on them and start reading till work time is over. This stops you from engaging in conversations that last a lot longer than you anticipated. One reply can turn into a phone call and before you know it, you've just wasted an hour. There's a time and place for everything and when you need to work you need to work, focus on nothing else then that.

It also acts like a little reward. I look forward to going through all my messages and chats as I'm connected to a bunch of groups and we converse daily about random things. They're fun and keep me socially active which is important when you work for yourself. By keeping myself from looking at them, I build the anticipation and I just push through work as fast as I can, sprinting at the end so I can read my messages.

Another important fact is that, every time you succumb to a distraction, no matter how small it is, it takes your mind some time to readjust to your mental work zone. The zone that allows you to work at 100% efficiency. Right now I've been writing for more than 30 minutes straight and words are just flowing. I feel like I'm a human type writer right now and have been able to type out almost 2,000 words in that short 30 minutes!

If I had checked a message here and there, it would have taken a good 2-4 minutes off every time as my mind had to readjust from activity to activity.

Moral of the story, enjoy your social media but keep it till the end. People will call you multiple times if they really need you.

Doing One New Thing First

This is something I recently started doing. Once you start having a business process that starts working for you, you'll begin to have a part of you that want's to constantly try new things. We're entrepreneurs, spotting opportunities is acting on new opportunities is half the reason we do this.

With this in mind, you'll start to notice that you'll have a big list of things to try one day. If this is you then make it a point to do one new thing every day. The trick is to do it <u>first</u>. If you're currently running an Instagram business and your main focus is to grow your Instagram following then over time you might find yourself listing things like,

- Try Instagram advertising platform
- Pay for a shoutout
- Try a share for share post with another Instagram user
- research on how to grow your Instagram quicker.
- Etc, etc

Try do one of these FIRST. This way you get it out of the way and your body will still force you to work on the general maintenance of your Instagram account as its what your mind knows to do best.

I've been doing this for 2 weeks now and have been slowly moving down the list. My list of 20 things to try and implement has dropped down to less than half. I've decluttered my mind and with each thing ticked off the list, it's made me more and more focused on what I need to do.

Try it out, it worked for me very well and i'll probably keep using it for years.

Working Down the List

This is something I picked up from my manager at my last job. I worked right next to him so was I would always observe how he got so much work done.

I used to be the type to make a big 'to do' list on excel and work on whatever I wanted, switching in between tasks if I got too bored of one. This way, I'd progress a little bit here and there but it would take me ages to complete a full task and tick it off as 'done'. In some cases a whole day would go by and I would still have the same to do list unchecked but a bit of progress has been made with each one.

My manager on the other hand would make the same to do list but would work on the first task until it was completely finished. He'd close all unrelated programs and work windows so his mind would focus 100% on this and in the same 8 hours I did my shift, he would have knocked a good 5-8 tasks off his list.

It was amazing how much of a difference it made. It almost looked like I did nothing compared to him.

When you work on a task your mind starts to become more and more in tune with it and will thoughts, actions and general parts of your body necessary to complete that task will start to flow naturally. As you progress, you build momentum and 20-30 minutes in you'll be immersed in it.

When you switch yourself to something else, you reset this momentum. It's like when you stop a rolling ball that's rolling down a hill at full speed. Once you let it go, it starts to roll really slowly until it builds momentum and is back to its speedy self. This is what happens when you switch to another task even it's picking up the phone to see if anyone has messaged you or to check your Instagram account. This is why when I work on a task now, I don't look at anything else until I work right through it.

For example, right now, I'm writing this book. Today I'd like to get 2,000 words written and so I won't stop for a break till I've done the whole 2,000. 20-30 minutes in I would have reached a natural rhythm I'm happy with and words just seem to flow off these fingers as I type. Switching to something else or picking up my phone to watch a short youtube clip will set me back more then just the 5 minutes it takes for me to watch the clip. It will probably set me back another 2-5 minutes of being in the adjustment phase.

Since I adjusted and started implementing this technique my productivity has increased ten fold. See, the main reason we don't get things done is because we rarely follow through 100% with the project. Most of my projects would remain unfinished. I had no one to blame but myself and I could never get past the 'uninterested' phase.

With almost everything you start, there will be times you will question your resolve. The boost of motivation you had when you first thought of the idea will start to lessen. This is where your need to be able to switch yourself to robot mode and push through all those doubts and negativities.

It took me a whole 2 months to make my youtube tutorial video collection for Selling merchandise on FaceBook marketing. I had sold over 600k worth of stock so I knew I had some great info to offer. It was a long and daunting task but I knew that once I finished, my blog traffic would increase tremendously. I doubted I could do this many times throughout the process but when these doubts entered my mind, I would just switch it to robot mode, put some music on, take a short break and great right back into it. I'd just keep moving forward.

I went from working on 5 random projects at a time to just focusing on getting things done one at a time. This enabled me to finish my tasks, take my learning and apply it to the next project, each time bettering my chances of success.

I would say this tactic of working down the list one task at a time was the biggest contributor to my productivity. It's a small tweak but makes a massive difference. The most important thing is <u>it got me to finish things.</u>

Timing Yourself/Putting the Timer on

This is a neat little hack I found somewhere online. I try and implement at least one thing I find online instead of reading '10 tips on bettering yourself' and forgetting them the next day.

This small tip was easy to implement but it does something interesting to your mind.

It's basically just putting the timer on for how long you think it will take you to finish a certain task and trying to get the task done within that time.
Right now, I'm writing this book and am aiming to write 2,000 words. I've set the timer for 1 hour and have mentally committed to try finish this task before the timer rings. Is it an easy task? Not really. Even though I can type all this out on the fly because I've done all of them, it's still a fast time for anyone to write 2,000 words.

This is the beauty of the tip though. It switches your mind into overdrive and makes you insanely focused on finishing it. Every time you think about picking up the phone or walking to the pantry to find some food or quickly switching on the tele and seeing what's on or taking a quick look on your Facebook/Instagram account, your mind will immediately knock the thought out of your head as it's convinced that you simply don't have the time to do it.

It's the same mentality rush I'd get during assignment submission at University. I'd have to submit an assignment at say 5pm. My body would be rushing to finish it by that time. Everything else would come secondary. Eating, returning a phone call, anything that would lessen the chances of me submitting my assignment on time would be completely ignored and it's only after 5pm, my mind would stabilise and I'd go do the things I needed to do.

You can start this anytime you want. Just turn on your timer every time you start a task. Make an intention before you start to complete this specific task before the timer runs out. You can even set it small to 20 minutes. Make sure you're specific with the goal you want to achieve so you can measure your success after. Like my goal of finishing 2,000 words of this book. At any time I can do a quick word count check and make sure I'm on time. Other tasks you can use it on can be,

- Spend 20 minutes reading up on Instagram

Marketing
- Spend 30 minutes writing a rough draft of a blog post
- 20 minutes to post a job on elance
- 15 minutes to clean your room

You can use it for anything in your life. The main idea here is to trick your body to focus. It doesn't really matter if you finish the task or not, you'll notice when you put the timer on, your mind just works faster and is more focused on what's in front of it.

Eating Healthy

I was never a big advocate of eating healthy. In fact I was quite the opposite. Big meals at work and McDonalds every day at university I didn't really think about it too much.

I've always been a hard gainer when it comes to putting on weight. I used to be the small skinny kid at school that would think he ate a lot but would never put on weight. For this reason it never occurred to me to question what I ate. I knew people get health problems but that's only when they're old right? Wrong. You can get healthy problems at anytime in your life.

I've learnt your body is stronger than you think but it's also fragile in certain aspects. Eating healthy is more then just maintaining your weight. Yes it does matter how you look and perceive yourself. There's no better confidence booster then looking and feeling good about yourself.

In saying all that eating healthy does many other things to your body that you can never experience until you eat healthy yourself.

A few years ago when I first began working for myself I was obsessed with trying new things to boost productivity and generally learn things about my body. A friend of mine found a diet called the 'raw vegan diet' when searching online and naturally I thought I'd join in with him for a few weeks jus for the fun of it. I didn't need to lose weight at all but I loved trying new things at the time so I went ahead with it.

For 3 weeks straight not a single processed food went into my system. Nothing cooked, nothing microwaved, ONLY raw fruits, vegetables and nuts. I'd make smoothies, juices, salads, soups made by blending mushrooms or sweet potato, plates of fruits, balls of nuts, dates and dried apricots, etc. The first week was ridiculously hard. It was like I had an addiction to meat, every time it came in front of me, it would take a tremendous amount of will power and effort to stop myself from eating or ordering any of it. I didn't really feel much changes inside of me. Maybe my body was still cleansing itself.

The second week was more or less the same except the cravings disappeared. A few times I was tested with really tasty cooked meals at restaurants and at home and I had been able to stick with the plan and make myself a fruit salad or smoothie instead.

The third week however was the <u>most amazing week I've ever had in my life</u>. I'm not exaggerating here. The week was full of energy. I never felt lethargic and had a constant pull to get outside and go do something in the sun. To dress nice and go shopping with friends and basically enjoy life. There seemed to be a connection with eating this way and the universe. It was as if I had tapped into a secret frequency of energy that only I was experiencing. I felt great about myself, my skin was becoming lighter, any blemishes or pimples I had began to clear up, my hair was getting stronger, muscle pains from gym would be gone the next day, my stamina was through the roof, the list of benefits are too long to list here.

Most importantly, it had me jumping out of bed at 5am ready to work on my business. I'd do 4-5 hours of work with no problem, finish at around 10am when everyone in the world is probably just settling into work and would be ready to do whatever I wanted in the day.

Eating healthy didn't just improve my productivity it tremendously improved my life quality. Right now I have only fruits and vegetables except I'll cook my veggies into a nice soup and mix in some canned beans. The rest of my meals will consist of smoothies, juices, protein balls and fruits. I make sure I get my macro requirements, (carbs, fats and proteins), and the necessary caloric requirements my body needs to be healthy. The only difference is that the quality of food going into my body is much better than what it used to be.

This is more a lifestyle change then a quick tip. Start off improving your breakfasts. There's nothing better than starting your day on the right foot. Make yourself a healthy smoothie, a platter of fruit, some juice or whatever you feel comfortable with. Once you get this routine down, move on to lunch and then slowly dinner. Keep at it for a month or two and I promise you, you'll feel a totally different person.

I would walk around feeling lethargic 24/7 always feeling to lazy to do anything. Waking up early was hard and I'd always feel like I wanted to go back to sleep. Now, I wake up at 5.30 and sleep at 11. My body doesn't even let me nap in the afternoons, I have too much energy for that.

Try it out, eating healthy should be one of your top priorities in life.

Finishing Activities Before a Certain Time

This is kind of like the timer tip I mentioned before but is more for the full working period.

When I worked, I considered myself pretty productive at times. Sure, there were times where I lazed around on the internet or took extra long on my lunch breaks but there were other days where I worked a whole 10 hours with no lunch break as I had way too much to do.

I thought this would be me when I worked by myself. I thought I'd be able to set a 'to-do list' on a note and work through it the whole 8 hours like we do at work. This was definitely not the case. Productivity was difficult and motivation came and went whenever it wanted to.

You see, when you're at work you have work pressure to keep you going. You may not think and reflect about it everyday but the reality is that if you didn't do your job for a week straight, you'd most likely get the boot at work. When you work for yourself and do nothing for a week straight there's no real immediate consequences. You just haven't moved forward.

This is where you need to be able to trick your mind. This tip works great and can be implemented everyday. Tell yourself that your only going to do work up till 5pm. No work after that. Your not allowed to open your laptop or your phone and do ANYTHING word related. It may sound counterproductive at the start but again, it's about tricking your mind to get to a certain state. When you do this and follow through with it, you'll find yourself wanting to ensure you get certain tasks done before your work time is over. Your mind won't have the luxury of telling itself that this task can be done later. It will stop continuously postponing things.

This used to happen to me a lot. The biggest reason I wouldn't get much work done is because I'd tell myself, 'I'd do it later'. It would be 11pm and I'd finally accept that I was not going to do this task and would just go to sleep repeating the process the next day. This technique is a counter to that mentality.

What we're doing is emulating the work environment. I know we all want the luxury of doing things whenever we feel like it but work is work and when you need to get things done, you get it done.

You don't have to set it at 5pm. I have it 10am in the morning. This way, I'm forced to wake up early and get right into work and finish what I can by 10am. Just by setting this for myself, I'm also forced to sleep early as I know I have to get up early for work.

Try it out and remember the most important things is to _follow through with it._Actually stop yourself at 10am or 5pm. Switch your laptop off no matter what task you're doing, not a single minute more. You'll find this frustrating at the start but as you adjust to it, you'll start doing all your tasks before the necessary times and consequently become much more productive.

Doing Certain Activities in Set Time Slots

This tip is similar to the above except it's broken down further to different activities and different times during the day.

I remember being in school and having 6 subjects to go through over a 6 hour day. Over the course of the semester we would have learnt a great deal about each subject. Can this be applied to business? Kind of.

When we're at school we have a start and end time for each subject. We can't do our Geography classwork in Math Class. Well, technically you can but then you'd fall behind in Math. At school, the start and end time meant that we had to finish everything for that class IN that class and also in the specific time slot. If not, we fall behind, get in trouble, get homework and all the stuff we don't like. In other words we get 'punished' and I use that word lightly.

Working for yourself means, in most cases, you'll have to emulate scenarios that make you productive. You CAN use the same school principal at home as long as you STOP doing that task at the end time and move on to the next task.

Here's how a sample of it would look.

8:00-10:00am – Activity One, (Write 2,000 words for Kindle)
11:00 – 1:00pm – Activity Two, (Make 2 Blog posts/Experimental Activities)
2:00 – 4:00pm – Activity Three, (Launch Campaigns for CPA Marketing)

The activities in brackets is what a sample day would look like for me. The idea here is to ONLY allow yourself to work on the activities in the allocated time slots. For example you can't start on Activity Two before 11:00am and your not allow to continue with it after 1:00pm.

Conditioning yourself to work this way will force you to be VERY productive within those hours since your mind knows it can't really do it 'later'. I mentioned this somewhere above but the main reason your mind delays tasks is because it believes or at least tricks itself into believing that it will do this particular task later. Most of use have around 14 hours in the day right? It shouldn't be too hard to do it later right? Wrong. The reason your mind wants to do it later is because it doesn't enjoy or like that task.

There will be many things in business that are very important but you just don't enjoy doing them. There's no special way to do anything, it just comes down to hard work and grinding it out. I know many 10k/day+ affiliate marketers and the only difference between them and those that make a few hundred a day is that they work hard. They do the same thing, but do a lot more than the hundreds/day guys. A lot of it is tedious tasks. Designing ads and banners, writing ad copy, finding targets, keywords, interests to bid on, etc, but it needs to be done.

This mind will stop your mind from tricking itself. It has no choice but to do it in that time slot or you miss out on doing that activity till the next day. For people like me that want to see progress in their business, it's very frustrating to not be able to work on what you know you need to work on. This itself is punishment.

Follow through with this if you want. It's a good one. I would recommend not to do TOO many tasks. You don't want to be applying yourself in 10 different business ideas/day because the rate of progression will be slow. It's better to just do 2 business ideas or even ideally 1 and break it into different tasks. For example for my blog I have to,

- Find new ways to market it
- Find and network with people to share ideas
- Respond to comments and emails
- Work on blog maintenance activities
- Write blog posts
- etc etc

My blog business has enough activities to keep me busy during the day and I can easily allocate different time slots for different sets of tasks. This is better when compared to doing completely different business ideas during the day.

Separating Different Ideas on Different Days

Now if your the type that just can't hold back from implementing a bunch of different business ideas all at the same time then you can try this technique.

If your brain is cluttered with a bunch of different business ideas, most likely you'll work on ideas here and there but will never commit to anything till you make it work. Every two days you'll get another idea and start on that too. This is real bad for focus and it's rare to find someone successful with this type of mentality.

What you need to do is be less cluttered and one way to do that is to allocate different business ideas for different days.

Let's say you have two business ideas. One is a blog, the other is a drop shipping website. Allocate Mondays, Wednesdays and Fridays to your Drop Shipping website and Tuesdays and Thursdays to your blog. You can try any day sets that work well with you. Maybe dedicate the first 3 days of the working week to business idea one and the last two days to business idea two. This way you'll be focussed on just one thing for the day which will insanely increase your productivity and stop you from jumping from one thing to another. Remember you lost time in switching from activity to activity so it's better to work on one thing till it's finished.

Decluttering your mind is important when it comes to achieving what you desire. Especially for entrepreneurs like us who are usually buzzing with ideas, if we don't know how to manage all these and act on them we'll just be a bank of good ideas. There's too many of those people around. Work on building techniques to optimise your output of these ideas, that's what real entrepreneurs do.

The 4-2 Hour Split

This is another idea for people that have multiple business ideas. I don't blame you guys, I always have business ideas running through the back of my mind and if I ever seriously want to dedicate my time to experimenting on them, this is what I do.

I usually allocate 4 – 6 hours to my business depending on what I do for the rest of the day. You can dedicate 4 hours to your main project and 2 hours to your side project. That's basically it. The important thing here however is to ONLY work on your main project in the 4 hour window and the side or experimental project during the 2 hour window.

Remember, forcing yourself to work in certain time slots forces you to make the most of your time.

You can do any split you like. I choose 4 and 2 because most of my time should really be spent on my main project and a small amount on experimental ideas. Why? Because in most cases your main project is your bread and butter. It's what you're seeing progress in and what's making you money. Keep building on what's already working, it's silly to switch it up before maximising profits from your main project.

In saying that, working on the same thing over and over again can tire you out and the repetitiveness can become real boring. For this reason it's healthy to have a side project to work on a well as long as you're smart with time allocation.

Doing a Minimum of 4 Hours a Day

When I first started working for myself, I had no idea how many hours is a good amount of time to work on your business every day. At work I was doing 8-10 hour shifts so I thought this is probably the best way to go about things.

I'd work the whole day, never really switching my brain off. Even if I was doing something completely different like hanging out with friends or spending time with family at a restaurant, my mind would be on the edge, constantly thinking about business.

I started to become a bit more smarter. I decided to think about things and break down how many hours the average person works on their business.

If your take the average office job or white collar profession in general, you'll realise that 4 hours of 100% productivity is PLENTY of work. It's more than what most successful entrepreneurs do. I'm not talking about 4 hours of general work. I'm talking about 4 hours of work _that matters_ and is _uninterrupted_.

In the office we spend the first hour settling in, having coffees, talking to people around the office and generally preparing to get into something. We'll do maybe an hour or two of work and then engage in conversation again, (if we haven't done so already), Then it's lunch time. We'll take a half hour break, most of us will stretch this to an hour. After coming back it'll take us some time to settle back in to work again. Once we do, we'll work a couple more hours while chatting with people and before you know it people are leaving the office.

I'm sure there would have been plenty of chatting breaks, smoke breaks, coffee breaks, internet breaks, email breaks, phone breaks, and general down time.

When deconstructing my working hours as a graduate engineer who had a lot to do, I would work between 3-5 hours on an average day. Sure there were the 8-10 hours of straight hectic work but for the most part, 3-5 hours was a good productive day.

One of the biggest reasons I became a full-time entrepreneur is because there were a bunch of other things I wanted to achieve but work meant I had not time for them. I wanted to learn boxing,

I'm obsessed with the sport. I wanted to enjoy my spare time and enjoy it with my friend and family, keep fit, eat healthy, do the things that better my life. Spending 8-10 hours slaving away is just too much of a life sacrifice for me and I'm sure it's the same for many others.

Now, I work my 4 hours between 6-12am which leaves me with the whole day to do what I want. I'll take a short nap after work, then go for a jog, spend time with my family, prepare my healthy meals, relax a bit more, go train boxing at 5, come back at 7, eat, cool down and restart.

It's a healthy routine that keeps my business and personal life progressing and that's what matters to me the most.

Being Consistent is Better Then a Sprint

This is one of the biggest secrets to achieving anything in life.

For a long time I'd jump from one idea to another. I'd spend 8-10 hours on this idea I was so obsessed with at the time and then totally burn myself out never wanting to it again.

A perfect example is when I first learnt about SEO and niche sites. For anyone that doesn't know what that is I'll explain it really quickly.

SEO stands for Search Engine Optimisation. It's basically optimising where google ranks you in their search results so you can appear as close to the top as possible when someone does a search on a particular keyword.

When I search 'work desks' in Google, Google will go through all the website pages in it's data base and give me what it thinks to be most relevant. In most cases it would have gone through 10s of thousands of pages to do this. How do you make YOUR website to be the one that comes up right at the top which gives you the highest chance of getting people to click on your website? This is where SEO comes in and it's a TONNE of writing and clever keyword placement.

That's how it used to be for me when I first got into it 5 years ago. I'd spend the whole day pumping out articles after articles about my product and then linking to them all over the net. I was obsessed with making this work and just wanted to see money coming in. My friend had made $100+ and if he could do it, I was convinced I could to. A couple of weeks later, I started to see some money trickling in. $2-$4 days. It was amazing, I thought I had broken through and continued to pump out articles.

I wrote at least 50 articles between 500 to 1,000 words in the course of a few weeks. Over time, my productivity started to slow down and even though I had made insane progress at the start, it just wasn't sustainable. I knew I could keep going if I forced myself but when your feeling like your forcing yourself, it's just a matter of time till you give up.

That's exactly what happened. I did it for a month straight and was so burnt out from the whole ideal, I couldn't bring myself to do it anymore. Even now when I think about SEO I cringe. It makes me feel giddy and I just hate the thought of writing so much about topics I have no interest in.

I started to learn it's better to pace myself. Instead of doing 50 hours of business a week for a few weeks and then needing to take a massive break, it's better to do 20 hours a week for months.

I don't feel like I need breaks at all, I can keep doing this for a full year.

It's good to be obsessive when the passion is there but try switch over to being consistent over a sprinter. A marathon runner will always run further than a sprinter and in business it takes a long amount of time spent in a certain industry to learn about it enough to make money with.

It took me 50 designs to get one to finally work with my Tshirt business. Most people get put off by that but if I hadn't continued with the first 50, I wouldn't have found that small success that allowed me to continue and eventually make over 6 figures that year.

Even with kindle publishing, most people will

make a book or two and then quit because they see no results. The smarter entrepreneur will make at least 10 and then re-evaluate how viable the business idea is.

If you have a high record of doing too much and eventually giving up, it's time you change your approach. Nothing beats being consistent, it's what gets you where you want to be. The patient man will always travel further.

Setting Goals for the Week Then Breaking Them Down Daily

How do you set your goals? Do you set them at all?

For a long time I'd make goals for the day and then just try and complete them. Most of the time, there would just be too much to do. I just had this overwhelming need to do ALL the tasks on my to do list on that day. In most cases I'd take breaks here and there and I'd be lucky to tick 2-3 tasks off.

I once conducted an experiment to actually go ahead and finish every task on my list. I wanted to know how much I was deceiving myself thinking this way. It took me 12 hours+ to do all the tasks and I realised how silly it was to put everything on the one to do list and try do it all in a day.

After that experiment I started thinking differently. Instead of making a to do list for the day, I made a list for the week. I sat there and thought about what I'd like to accomplish for the week. After I was happy with it, I'd go further and break it down for each day.

This way, I realised I don't need to do much to achieve my daily and weekly goal. It was satisfying enough to know that I'll get these tasks done during the week instead of that day.

The problem I had before was planning way too short term. I never looked ahead and contemplated on what level of productivity and achievement would make me happy. I never planned ahead and worked backwards. I would always keep planning for the day and continue to move in a direction I had no idea where it was going.

Many times we feel like we can be insanely productive as we plan to do a bunch of things in our minds. We feel like we're accomplishing things by listing down our plan of attack, making mock ups and more planning. When it comes to sitting down and actually doing the work, that's where most people drop out. When you accept this is the more likely outcome you can start training yourself to be as productive with your action as your during the planning stages.

This is a technique that definitely helps with that

so again, if you're the planning type, try make a list of things you'd like to achieve for the week and then break them down daily. Don't overwhelm yourself and put in 3 months worth of work for one week, be realistic. Make a list, then half it. Do the first half in one week and the second half in the other week. The most important thing is it should be _DOABLE._ It's better to take 3 weeks to _finish_ a set of tasks then it is to go hard for a week and then giving up, never really completing the set of tasks at all.

Saying No/Sacrifice

No successful entrepreneur got to where they wanted without a great deal of sacrifice.

I always get annoyed at people that think we have it easy because we work for ourselves. They think we do barely anything and are the fortunate, 'lucky' few that have it good. No one sees the amount of stress behind what it took from the beginning. The days spent pushing ourselves in the late hours of the night when every inch of our body was screaming at you to give up.

It's overwhelming, more so than work.

At the start of all this, I'd be doing everything. I'd be seeing friends, taking up boxing, reading, working on my business, learning arabic, and a bunch of other things. I'd be a 'yes' man. It's great to be a yes man, you learn a lot of things and life takes you places you never thought you'd get to but when your starting off in business you have to learn to say no.
No, I can't go on that 2 week holiday to Sydney with you.

No, I don't need to go to meetups to share ideas, it's better to spend it grinding it out with my business.
No, I'm not available this weekend, I'm working on my business.

It took me a while to learn the importance of saying No. I'd say yes to everything, mostly because I felt rude saying no. I thought people would get offended and I'd make someone upset.

I realised that I was spending a whole lot of time on things that were unnecessary. I found myself in places I didn't want to be just because I had said yes to someone.

Now I don't care. Well maybe I do, a little, but there's only so much time in the day and as an entrepreneur you have to be smart when spending it. Sure, you can do everything you want to do, but at a later time. At the early stages of business when you need to get something off the ground, it's best to work your schedules around that. Dedicate yourself to your business. Everything comes secondary. Make it your number one focus. Of course, spend time with your loved ones and on your health but don't say yes to everything.

Learn to say No and be confident saying it. You don't have to always say yes. You don't always have to help people. Help yourself first and put yourself in a mental state where you're happy and very able to help someone, then it will make for an enjoyable experience for both of you.

When I realised this, I had so much time for myself and my business. I could slot things in where every I wanted. My friends and family slowly adjusted to my schedule and eventually understood that there were just some times during the day that I was too busy.

Reward Right After

This one's a nice little tip to keep you chugging along during the day.

I like to work in a way where there are absolutely 0 distractions. The only thing that distracts me from time to time is my pet bird that will fly to my shoulder and start nibbling and playing around for a bit. I'll give him a pat and a cuddle and he'll be on his birdy way doing his birdy things. I can do it while still being focussed, it doesn't take much mental effort having him around.

Picking up my phone and checking my FaceBook however has a whole different effect. It changed my focus and takes my mind to a different place. I've discussed before where switching between tasks can waste your time in the 'adjustment' phase. For this reason, I work in short sprints.

Right now, I'm writing my kindle book so I'll keep going till I smash out 2-4000 words and then reward myself with a bit of a break later. I'll walk around, watch some youtube, get some food, watch some more youtube and half an hour to an hour later will be ready to go again.

Some people work 1 hour straight and take a 5 minute break. Whatever your sweet spot is, work to it.

During that hour, that 5 minute break or that small reward of watching an episode of your favorite TV show will keep you going. You'll get work done and give your mind some healthy play time so it can produce quality work again. Both are necessary for a healthy balance. Too much work and no play makes you miserable whereas too much play and no work gets you nowhere. When you learn to satisfy both aspects, you'll begin to be more consistent.

Grouping Tasks

Grouping tasks is an awesome way to get more things done. There's a couple ways to do this depending on what works best for you. Everyone is different so the exact way I do things might not work for someone else.

The way I group tasks is to group a really hard task with a couple of easy ones. The ideas is to get the easy tasks out of the way while you have the momentum gained from working through the big tasks.

When you stop working, it makes it harder to get back into it. By stopping after you feel like you've done something huge for the day, you will feel it much harder to flip open your laptop and spend 5-10 minutes on those tasks you still have listed in your to-do list.

This is why I just group them together. Even though I'm exhausted from completing something huge, my mind is still in productivity mode so it's best to use that energy to still continue accomplishing things.

You don't have to do it this way. You can simply group whatever tasks you feel like. Grouping tasks just makes it easier to accomplish more. It's a way to trick the mind into thinking that this set of tasks is still just the one task.

Half the time when you're working for yourself it's the mind you have to conquer. Almost everyone has the same physical limbs necessary to do the tasks required to build a business, they just have different minds. You need to train your mind into thinking a certain way. In a way that's different to working for a job. Once your mind has switched over to entrepreneur mode and can implement a variety of these techniques, you'll start to see constant progress and productivity.

Using Kanban

There are plenty of tools that people use to increase their productivity. From simple notepad that comes standard on every windows or MAC computer to Evernote. I personally use notepad and have been using it ever since I started with online marketing.

Many people however have sworn a productivity method called Kanban. If you have never heard of it don't worry I'll explain. It's a system the Japanese used to keep everything working on time and efficiently in their manufacturing/production industries. You may have used the concept at some stage of your life to properly plan and keep track of your progress.

Instead of placing your tasks in a 'list' type fashion, crossing them out as you go, you place them in different columns that represent different phases of the tasks life. Here it is in its most simple form,

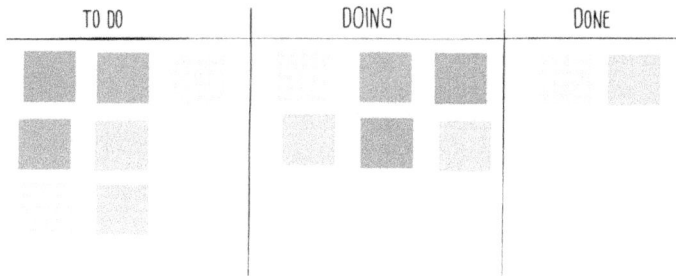

TO DO	DOING	DONE

This way, it gives you more of an outlook where your tasks are. If they're in the 'doing phase', it will motivate you to put it one step further and place it in the 'done' column.

Productivity, as I've mentioned before, is all about managing your mind. Everyone can be productive but you have to implement techniques and processes that sometimes trick the mind into working the way you want it. Kanban allows you to mentally feel more organised and move tasks systematically along the productivity process line. Some Kanban softwares get even more intricate such as the one below,

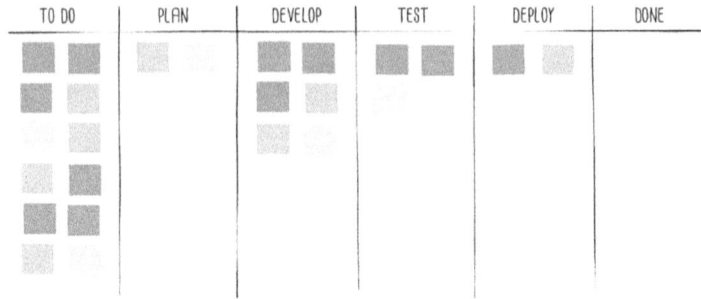

If you're working on projects, this might be better for you. It allows you to better manage your mind. There's no point having it all in your head, somewhere along the way things will get lost, and forgotten. Always make it a point to mind dump what's in your head so you can understand what you need to do to get to where you want to be.

One of the biggest issues with first time entrepreneurs is having too many things in their head. They have a short term and long term vision of owning 10 business and having a portfolio in 50 different companies. It's definitely possible to get there but if you're not able to systematically organise yourself where you can focus in on ONLY the task in front of you, then you'll never achieve anything. It's like trying to put a roof on a house that has no walls or brickwork. You look so far ahead, you're not willing to do the short term grinding that you need to do.

Tools like Kanban help to understand and manage that process. Every entrepreneur has done or still does tedious tasks that may be boring for others but they're effective. Sometimes you just need to force yourself to get it done.

If you want to try it out, search for kanbanflow. A few people use it in my industry and have been using it for over a year.

Measuring your Progress by Writing Down how Much you've Worked

Your mind is very good at deceiving itself. Being aware of this is the first step to properly manage it. Sometimes it's too optimistic, sometimes it's too pessimistic. It will tell you that you have plenty of time when you don't. On the other hand it will tell you continuously that you're not capable of great things when everyone is.

One way to keep it accountable is to write down your daily progress.

I had the problem of not getting tasks done because my mind would simply continue to delay them. Every time I'd get a small spark to start the task, I'd find some other distraction and tell myself I'll do it later. It would be 8pm and I'd still be telling myself this.

Start writing a daily diary for yourself if this is you or if you're the type to spend hours and hours 'working' but still have issues getting things done. Remember, your mind is a master at deceiving itself. Sometimes people sit a whole 8 hours on their work desk and get a couple of hours of real work done. They could have spent the other 6 hours playing warcraft and it would have given them the same result.

When I worked as a graduate Civil Engineer, I'd be working on projects along with a few others. We'd be switching between projects and some would have random weeks off due to holidays and being on a different project. The first thing we did when we got back into a project was to check our work diaries that the others had written. The diary entries would be very specific even down to the times that certain activities were started and ended. The diaries also gave insight into how much work had been done. While writing it I'll realise that I did a LOT of work or sometimes would realise I hardly did anything today.

This is the reason I'd keep a work diary for my personal life. If you can keep track of how much actual work you're getting done, what times your getting them done in, etc, you can start improving. It all comes down to being analytical and having data to go off. You can work for years on end diecieving yourself that you're being productive when at most you're working a couple of hours a day. This way, as long as you don't lie to yourself when writing things down, you'll know where improvements can be made and hopefully act upon them.

Make a simple excel spreadsheet and update it for a week straight. Have a look at it after and analyse your work habits. I'm sure there is plenty you can improve on.

Motivating Yourself Through Writing
Things you'd do when you Achieve your Goals'

This is one of the biggest things that work for me. Sometimes it's the fear of punishment that get people to be productive. Other times it's the excitement of reward. For many people it's both. I'm like this. Although setting punishments I'm actually afraid of gets me working quite hard, having a massive gift for yourself if you hit a certain task can also get you insanely motivated.

When I hit a certain goal, I make it a point to reward myself. For example, if I have a 10k profit month, I'll spoil my self with a $1,000 shopping spree. I'll deck myself out with some new clothes or new games and freely splurge because I've earned it. If I make over $100k this year, I'll buy my WRX the sti sports kit and rims. I've been wanting to get it so badly, it would look so awesome! It might cost 3-5k but again, I've earned it.

If I totally kill it and make over 300k, well I'm just going to upgrade my car to an R35 GTR. Why not? I've worked hard for it. We work to make our life better for ourselves. To improve the quality of our lives. There's not point working so hard when your lifestyle is going to stay the same.

BUT, you don't want to be overdoing it. I save 80%+ of my income. It goes straight to my bank account or towards my low risk investment funds. This way, I only splurge on myself when I've earned it. If you're going to throw money around everywhere then it'll eventually be like you never earned it at all. There's no point Earning 500k and spending 480k. You might as well get a job that pays you 20k. Don't increase your spending just because. I still have meals that cost me around $15- $25 max. I'm not going to spend money on

$50 meals just because I can afford it now.

If you don't balance your spending you'll feel poor no matter how much you earn but at the same time I don't believe in saving everything and not enjoying life.

If this technique works for you use it. Tell yourself you'll only buy a new game station, phone, gopro or whatever entices you only if you hit a certain goal with your business.

Becoming very Emotional about your Goal

I remember once I watched this video on Youtube where a bunch of thugs were beating the living day lights out of a young man. He had done nothing to them, looked very innocent and seemed to be just walking home. One of the aggressors video taped it, while him and his 5+ buddies kicked him punched him, beat him to the ground and continued to do so for at least 5 whole gruelling minutes.

That video effected me a lot. No way did I ever want to be in a position that I couldn't defend myself and no way would I stand by if I saw something like that happen in front of me. Since that day I've been insanely obsessed with martial arts. I watch UFC fights and boxing fights all the time. It's become my main hobby and my eating and fitness habits revolve around me getting better at boxing.

Just from that one video clip, it changed my whole outlook on a sport I was never interested in.

A similar situation happened when I quit work the first time. My friends were all moving ahead with their financial life, working hard, saving and some even buying houses. I could have been doing the same if I continued with work but I decided to take the sacrifice and learn business even if it would set me back in the short term.

The thought of being left behind killed me. It was what woke me up in the mornings and got me straight into work for the next 10 hours. My savings account was steadily depleting and with every passing month I was getting more and more desperate to make it work. My bank account was getting closer and closer to zero and it was only a matter of time till I had to go back to work. But then I decided to never go back to work. To not care if my bank account hit zero or if I was on the streets I didn't care anymore. I was going to make this work no matter what. The emotion and drive was so intense I would work the whole day hardly eating anything or talking to anyone. I was getting a lot done and learning so much. Looking back, it wasn't a healthy lifestyle balance but when your emotions get firmly attached to your life goals to the point you don't care about anything else, goals start being achieved.

What initially started with a curiosity for business and an attempt to start one while living the life I wanted to live, eventually turned into a desperate struggle to make it work no matter what. I changed from just focusing on it on the side to making it my one and only priority in life.

This same scenario plays out in everyones life who has ever been successful at anything. At some point they've been desperate to achieve it. It's dominated their thoughts to the point nothing else mattered.

These days I have a steady business and am not as desperate or as hungry as I used to be. In saying that I can definitely bring back that emotion by doing a few crazy things. I can give my friend 30k and tell him that if I ever report to him that I did less than 6 hours of work on any given work day then he MUST donate it to a charity I hate the most. I can assure you I'd be working my 6 hour days.

Emotions can be generated artificially or they can come from genuine experiences. Whether it's hate, love, anger, insecurities or whatever that's driving you, learn to channel it into the right direction.

If it's anger, channel it into a martial arts club, go to the gym, work on your body, show the world and whoever your angry at you can live a great life without them. If it's love, spread it fairly. Use it in ways to motivate you to do what it takes to achieve your financial goals.

You'll have to force yourself at the start. It's natural to sulk over things on your couch and feel like you don't have the energy to do anything. No one every woke up 100% ready to start a business or a gym membership. There's always a bit of effort required to push the boulder so it starts rolling but once it's rolling fast, it's hard to stop

Conclusion

There are plenty of techniques here to go through. You don't have to use them all to be successful but you definitely have to implement some.

I would recommend going down the list one-by-one and see what works for you. You might stop at the first one and find yourself insanely more productive!

As long as this book has been able to help you improve the amount of quality time you spend on your business, it's done it's job.

Keep grinding and hustling towards your goal, implement the necessary habits and systems regardless of how bizarre they are or what anyone else thinks of them. Remember, it's YOUR dream and no one can get you there but yourself.

Good luck!

- Mateen

www.ingramcontent.com/pod-product-compliance
Lightning Source LLC
Chambersburg PA
CBHW061445180526
45170CB00004B/1568